Master Of 'ME'

मेरा पहला कदम

Collection of English & Hindi Poems

Vaishali Nayak

BookLeaf
Publishing

India | USA | UK

Made with ❤ on the BookLeaf Publishing Platform
www.bookleafpub.in
www.bookleafpub.com

Dedication

I dedicate this book to my late father, Shri Vasant Anant Sangurdekar, whose untimely demise left a deep void in our hearts and our lives. Being an avid reader himself, he always encouraged us, his two daughters, to inculcate good reading habits. His love for good writing with a strong vocabulary found a valuable niche in a segment of a well-known newspaper. This book aims to give a profound tribute to his values and his beliefs in the power of expression through writing works.

I also dedicate this book to all my students, who have been my hidden strength and motivation for all my new initiatives and ventures. Interacting with them has always been an enriching experience for me.

Preface

This book, comprising varied-theme based English and Hindi poems with their summaries, appeals to all age groups of the society and is easy to understand. This novel piece of work depicts relationship not only with our dear ones but also with our material objects. Some of the subject matters may turn out to be surprise for you !! The poems in this book, based on different shades of emotions, will inspire you, make you laugh, revive your lost connections, make you feel grateful and much more. This worth-reading experience will make you go through this book multiple number of times and will emerge you feeling motivated, cheerful, and energetic.

I always believed that poems are the most effective form of expression, and this led me to write my debut book of poems, thus satiating my quench of love for writing. This precious writing period has been a fulfilling and enriching experience for me in all my domains of development.

Acknowledgements

First and foremost, I would like to deeply thank the Almighty for giving me well-fortified strength in my writing journey. On an equal level, I express my profound gratitude to the pillars of my life, my mother, Smt. Varsha Vasant Sangurdekar, and my spouse, Mr. Ramnath Purandar Nayak, for being my sturdy motivators in carrying out this writing work with zeal and enthusiasm.

I will always be indebted to my late father, Vasant Anant Sangurdekar, who sowed in me the seed of love for reading and writing. Many thanks to my family and well-wishers who have always stood by me as my constant support. Special thanks to my younger son Mst. Anuj Nayak for his assistance on cover designing part of this book.

My sincere thanks to my publisher for giving me this wonderful opportunity as a challenge and then making my dream piece of writing work available across the world through different mediums.

Master of 'ME'

Mirror Mirror on the wall
Who is the Master of All?
Everyone wants to know
But can this help us to grow?

Ego, hate and envy surround us
How to survive among thus
Facing them with presence of mind
Can make us bold, wise and kind

Love and peace across the world
Can keep the bonds of lives furled
Master of World desires everyone to be
But soon I realised
It should be 'Master of ME'

Summary -
In today's modern times, humans have many negative aspects around them. At times, facing them may be challenging and overwhelming. Most of us struggle to overcome these by trying to change others and land up in despair. This poem advises that instead of expecting the world to change, we can change our outlook and

focus on self-growth and development. Mastering oneself will ultimately lead the world towards love, peace and positivity.

मेरा पहला कदम

चलते चलते जब मैं थक जाता हूँ
याद आता है वह मेरा पहला कदम,
चुपके से कहता है मुझसे वह
अब खुद पर कर ले थोड़ासा रहम।

बढ़ते कदम तो लगते हैं सुहाने
पर रुक कर थोड़ा तू ,
इधर-उधर नजर डाले
सुन ले इस प्रकृति की पुकार
कहता है वह मेरा पहला कदम
खुशी कर ले खुद पर न्योछार।

थकना कमजोरी का नाम नहीं है
सोच ना तू, तुझ में कुछ कमी है ,
चलना रूकना यही जीवन का नाम
कहता है वह मेरा पहला कदम
काम का ना बन तू गुलाम ।

सारांश

आजकल की भागदौड़ के जीवन में आदमी इतना उलझ गया है कि
वह खुद की ओर देखना भूल गया है। यह कविता आदमी को उसके
जीवन के हर एक क्षेत्र के पहले कदम की याद दिलाती है, जो उसने
धीरे-धीरे लिया था। लेकिन वही आदमी आज तेजी से बढ़ने की चाह

में थोड़ी देर रुकने से डरता है। इस कविता द्वारा यह सलाह दी गई है कि थोड़ी देर रुकना कमजोरी नहीं, बल्कि होशियारी है।

Little Hands,Strong Minds

A child is like a butterfly
Some bold and some shy
Each one with its unique colours
As if the garden full of flowers

The budding young mind steadily blooms
With every gentle touch, right from the womb
The vehemence of the emotions grows
Just as the earthly blue water flows

With lots of questions on their endearing face
Foster it with love, warmth and grace
Hop and jump and their naughty run !!!
Enlivens the energy with lots of fun

'Little hands' desires a tender fair hold
Soon their 'Strong minds' gradually unfold
Let us accept them as they are !
And watch them spread their wings afar

Summary
As rightly stated in the proverb, "A child is the father of
a man," an adult is the outcome of his childhood
experiences and journey. This poem conveys a message

to the parents that just like flowers have their characteristics and are different from each other, the same way their children are distinct from others in many ways, and they should be accepted wholeheartedly, which will help them to bloom as a unique, strong identity.

हमारा रखवाला

चाहे हो तपती धूप, चाहे हो सख्त सर्दी
हम नभचर आस लिए बैठे हैं,
वह कोमल हाथों की नरमी ।

कभी सहलाता, कभी घोंसले बनता
अनाज के दाने जमीन पर बिखरता,
जल की कटोरी हाथ में लिए
ढूंढते हमें उसके आँखों के दिए,
देख हमें, उसके चेहरे की वह मुस्कान
हमारे रखवाले तुझ पर हमारा जीवन कुर्बान ।

देर बहुत हो गई है ,
बेसब्री भी बढ़ने लगी है
कहाँ रह गया हमारा पालनहार ,
पंख पसारे हम हैं तैयार ।

लो,आई उन कदमों की आहट
उसके मधुर वाणी से हुई जगमगाहट ,
अचानक से पर फड़फड़ाने लगे
निर्भयतेसे रखवाले की और बढ़ने लगे ।

सारांश

मानव और पक्षियों का नाता बरसों पुराना है। इस प्रेम के बंधन को
दर्शाते हुए यह कविता रची गई है। पक्षियों को जैसे अपने रखवाले की

आदत सी हो गई है और आज उसके न आने पर वे चिंतित हो रहे हैं। रखवाले के आने की आहट से उनका मन प्रफुल्लित हो जाता है और वे उसकी ओर बढ़ते हैं। पक्षियों की अपने रखवाले के प्रति व्याकुलता और उसके लिए उनकी कृतज्ञता बड़े सुंदर शब्दों से इस कविता में प्रस्तुत की गई है।

The Teacher in Me

Call it a passion or a profession
Under my wings, young precious possessions
Being among them - is the magical key
That's what says 'The Teacher in Me'

Innocent looks with vibrant hope
Creative ideas in me, invoke
Adore these buds blossom on your tree
That's what says 'The Teacher in Me'

With discussions, forum and debates
For my little wonders to rejuvenate
Listen to them with lots of glee
That's what says 'The Teacher in Me'

Love and care with gentle discipline
Cheer them up to think and imagine
Let these minds feel carefree
That's what says 'The Teacher in Me'

Summary
Children are considered to be the future of their nation. The onus of shaping them into responsible citizens lies in the hands of a teacher. This poem explores the gradual

unveiling of a teacher's mind through each and every interaction with the students. The teacher realizes that along with the scholastic growth, it is her duty to help her students to express themselves by ways of different outlets, contributing to the emotional development of the students.

पेड़ लगाओ

अपने भारतवर्ष को हम स्वर्ग बनायेंगे
पेड़ लगायेंगे, फल फूल उगायेंगे।

धरती ने जन्म दिया , पाला-पोसा पौधों ने,
लेकिन मतलब के लिए इनको तोडा लोगोंने
अब इनको ना कोई हम नुकसान पहुँचायेंगे
पेड़ लगायेंगे , फल फूल उगायेंगे।

कर्ज चुकाने का मिला है यह अच्छा मौका
पेड़ लगाओ, पेड़ लगाओ नारा हो सबका
खत पानी देकर हम अपना फर्ज निभायेंगे
पेड़ लगायेंगे, फल फूल उगायेंगे।

सारांश

मानव जाति अपने संसाधनों के लिए प्रत्यक्ष या अप्रत्यक्ष रूप से पेड़-पौधों पर ही निर्भर है। लेकिन स्वार्थ हेतु यही मानव आज वन कटाई में लगा हुआ है। इसका मानव जीवन के लिए नकारात्मक परिणाम हो सकता है। इस बात की ओर मानव का ध्यान खींचते हुए यह कविता रची गई है। इसी के साथ मानव को वनीकरण का संदेश देते हुए पेड़ों के प्रति उनका फ़र्ज़ निभाने की सलाह दी गई है।

My Travel Mate - Tata Nano

With the new daylight
The same question arise
Work and home, to and fro
I wonder how do I go

I wish I had a magical wand
To ask for some helping hand
And LO !!! My wish came true
My new Tata Nano came to my rescue

In my wallet goes, my driving permit
Enough for my confidence to be well-lit
My curious mind ask "How will driving feel?"
Whispered my Nano "Try it on my wheels"

Cautious and careful with every driving moves
Independent I am, my Nano now proves
Oh! my dear travel buddy, you made me smart
No matter how many cars I drive further
You will forever remain in my heart

Summary
Modern working-class people find traveling to and fro from the office more exhausting than their office

workload. Public transport may not be developed in some areas, resulting in most of them opting for their vehicle. This humorous poem is about an individual finding his independence and confidence after learning to drive and owning his first car, the Tata Nano. Furthermore, this poem also conveys the gratitude of the individual for his vehicle, which remains deeply rooted in his heart.

माँ का अनुशासन

समय से उठाना, समय से सोना
समय से खाना और पीना
बचपन से ही माँ को दिखा
खींचते अनुशासन की रेखा ।

वक्त कभी रुकता नहीं
किसी के लिए झुकता नहीं
वक्त के दायरे में रहना
माँ से ही सीखा वक्त का आदर करना ।

हर कार्य में माँ की स्थिरता
योग, ध्यान, प्राणायाम की निरंतरता
कभी ना उसके रुकते कदम
कहते हैं चलते रहना हरदम ।

नियम हो चाहे मन के या तन के
पालन करना जिम्मेदार बनके
राह पकड़ मेरी, आत्मनिर्भर बनो
कहता माँ का अनुशासन, अब मेरी यह बात सुनो ।

सारांश

जीवन की सफलता में अनुशासन एक अभिन्न हिस्सा है। बच्चों के लिए उनके माँ-बाप आदर्श व्यक्ति होते हैं। इस कविता में एक व्यक्ति अपनी माँ के नियमबद्ध आचरण को सराहते हुए अनुशासन का

महत्व बताना चाहता है। अपनी माँ से सीखा हुआ यह गुण वह अपने जीवन में समेट लेना चाहता है।

My Smart Grandma

With Redmi in her hand
Proud about her brand
I wonder with this digital art
"Grandma, Have you really become smart ?"

Browsing through the reels
Looking for shopping deals
Chatting with your friends
Blending with modern trends
Have drifted us both apart
I wonder, "Grandma, have you really become smart ?

Longing for your endless stories
Of bravery, valour and old glories
Ludo, cards and other board games
Remains now just for sake of names
Missing your bond deep in my heart
I wonder, "Grandma, Have you really become smart?"

Keeping your new friend aside
Can you sit with me beside?
Let me hear and let me say
Closer we come day by day
Let this golden ties regain

Then I can proudly say ,
 "My Smart Grandma is back again"

Summary

Mobile addiction has become common nowadays not only among youngsters but also elderly people. This has driven the old and young generations apart. This poem is about the plea of a small grandchild to his grandma for the latter's attention. The grandchild reminisces about the old memories with his grandma when the smartphone was not with her. He wants to regain those golden days so that he can get back the cherished interaction with his loving grandma.

10. गुरु

घर से बाहर कदम निकला
खुद को फिर अकेला पाया
माँ ने जिसका हाथ थमाया
वह व्यक्ति गुरु कहलाया।

हर मोड़ पर रास्ता दिखाया
मुझे पढ़ाया मुझे सिखाया
हर प्रश्न का उत्तर बतलाया
वह व्यक्ति गुरु कहलाया।

मेरी जिज्ञासा का ध्वज फहराया
मेरे गुण अवगुण को अपनाया
मेरे साथ सदा जिसका साया
वह व्यक्ति गुरु कहलाया।

सही गलत का फरक दिखलाया
ज्ञान से मेरा जीवन सजाया
मेरे नमन करते ही, जो मुस्काया
ऐसा महान व्यक्ति गुरु कहलाया

सारांश

हमारे जीवन में गुरु का एक महत्वपूर्ण स्थान है। हमारे गुरु हमें शिक्षा और दिशा प्रदान करते हैं। ऐसे महान व्यक्ति के गुणगान करते हुए यह

कविता रची गई है। गुरु को नमन करके उनका आदर करना हमारा परम कर्तव्य है।

Life partnership

In the cricket field of our marriage span
Holding hands, happy memories we scan
Love and togetherness of our innings
Let's celebrate our silver jubilee winnings

Entering on our marriage pitch
Facing each problem and other glitch
With every passing days, adding to our runs
Now proud parents of our young ones

Our life partnership stood the test of time
For both of us, it holds the value of prime
Neither bowled, stumped, caught and all
Let's ensure our wickets never fall

Summary

Marriages are made in heaven is rightly depicted in this poem. Using cricket as a metaphor, the loving partnership of a married life, completing silver jubilee years, is compared to the long-term partnership in a cricket innings. Whether it is cricket or married life, it requires a great amount of commitment and understanding to sustain the respective partnership.

Such partnerships add great value and become a sense of
pride.

21

कागज पे होली

आज मन में हुई कुछ बेचैनी
देखकर मेरी सूरत रोनी
बोल उठी रंगों की टोली
आज खेल तू कागज पे होली ।

बहुत समय के बाद हम मिले
हम दोनों के दिल है खिले
रंग से मेरा नाता अनोखा
धीरे-धीरे उसे उभरते देखा ।

रंगों को कागज से मिलवाया
इन रंगों ने मेरा मन सहलाया
उदासीनता ढलने लगी है
नई उम्मीदें जगने लगी है ।

सारांश

मानवी जीवन में रुचि या शौक एक महत्वपूर्ण हिस्सा है। अपने जीवन को मार्ग दिखाने के साथ-साथ यह एक तनाव निवारक भी है। आधुनिक मानव अपनी गड़बड़ी के जीवन में रुचियों को अनदेखा कर रहा है। इस कविता में एक ऐसे शौक,चित्रकारी, को पुनर्जीवित करने की बात की गई है। ऐसा करने पर जीवन में फिर से नई आशाएं और उम्मीदें जाग उठती हैं।

My Healthy Pathfinder

Munching on the chips, biting till they crack
Suddenly I heard my name from my side rack
With looks of surprise, left side I gazed
And found my weighing scale with its eyebrows raised

Scared I stood on it, with my eyes closed
Nervous did I felt and my mind decomposed
Roared my friend from below
And my pounding heart went flat
"Oh No !!! , You foolish lady, you have become fat."

Pizza, burger, chocolates sound tempting and delicious
Warned my weighing scale,
 better be mindful and conscious
With its frowning face were its constant reminders
Soon I went along with my new Pathfinder

Exercise, diet, yoga now my new routine
'Healthy weight loss' became my sweet dream
With passing days and months, my dream came true
My smiling weighing scale said
 "Good !!! finally you have got through."

Summary

In the present scenario, a sedentary lifestyle has become the cause of many health issues, obesity being one of them. With a tinge of humor, this poem personifies a material object—a weight monitor and, in a comical aspect, brings out the dialogue between it and its user. Weight loss in a healthier manner is emphasized and appreciated.

एक नारियल की कहानी

एक नारियल पेड़ से टपका
लुढ़क लुढ़क के झाड़ी में अटका
उसकी आवाज से सारे चौंके
अनेक पैर उसकी और दौड़े ।

बबलू बोला 'यह नारियल मेरा है'
फेक के पत्थर मैंने उसे तोड़ा है
सारे बोले बबलू तू झूठा है
ऐसे कभी किसीने नारियल तोड़ा है ?

'नारियल पर हक मेरा है' बोली नानी
इसके पेड़ को दिया है मैंने पानी
सारों ने नानी को घेरा
पूछा 'नारियल पर नाम लिखा है क्या तेरा?'

सारे नारियल की तरफ़ झपटे
पाया मोती कुत्ते को नारियल से लिपटे
भौंकने लगा, मोती भूख से मारे
दुम दबा के भाग गए सारे ।

सारांश

इंसान के पदार्थवादी स्वभाव के कारण वह छोटी-छोटी वस्तुओं के
लिए भी उसका मोह नियंत्रण में नहीं रख पाता है। यह हास्यास्पद

कविता इसी बात को दर्शाती है। एक पेड़ से टपके हुए नारियल के लिए इंसानों का मौखिक संघर्ष और हाथापाई, चाहे वह एक बच्चा हो या बुजुर्ग, इस कविता में विनोद शैली में प्रस्तुत की गई है।

Tiny night monsters

Deep in my night's sleep
After a long and tiring day
Came those tiny monsters
To attack my peaceful slumber

Humming through my earlobe
As irritating as it can
I wish I had a glue
To fix its mouth before it flew

Waking up in the mid of night
Rubbing my red sore eyes
I tried to crush it in my nasty clap
But swiftly escaped that naughty little chap

Cursing those little devils
I took oath not to spare them
Stumbling to grap my mosquito racket
And almost felt flat near my hanging jacket

Limping with the racket in hand
I started searching them all around
Thinking it's now or never

Those smarty rascals hid as if forever

Tired and exhausted on sofa I fell
Again that same humming sound as worse as hell

Summary -
After a long and tiring day, everyone yearns for a peaceful sound sleep at night. But what if a tiny creature, like a mosquito, tries to attack your slumber? This poem, with its generous dosage of humor, tries to bring out the frustration in such case. This also shows that during a night tussle between the two, even a relatively minute being like a mosquito can outsmart a human who is much more superior to him. So, no one should be considered inferior at any point.

दो परछाइयाँ

मानव रूप को छोड़ा है, धरती को नहीं
पीछे रह गई मेरी दो परछाइयाँ कहीं

आसमान से ढूंढते मेरी यह नम आँखें
करना चाहती है तुमसे ढेर सारी बातें

आज फूल बनकर खिली है मेरी दो कलियाँ
सक्षम होकर निभा रही है सारी जिम्मेदारियाँ

हमेशा प्रगति पथ पर चलते रहना
चाहे हो कोई भी ठोकर सहाना

देखना चाहता हूँ तुम्हें सदा पंख फैलता
मेरी बेटियों, तुम पर गर्व करता है तुम्हारा पिता

सारांश

पिता-पुत्री के प्यार के असीम बंधन को दर्शाती हुई यह एक भावनात्मक कविता है। असामयिक मृत्यु होने पर एक स्वर्गवासी पिता आसमान से अपनी दोनों बेटियों को अपनी पूरी जिम्मेदारियां निभाते हुए देखकर गर्व करता है। धरती पर उसकी दो बेटियाँ उसे अपनी ही परछाइयाँ लगती हैं। उन्हें आशीर्वाद देते हुए हमेशा बढ़ने की मंगलकामनाएं देता है।

Let me CRY !!

Be a son, be a brother
Be a husband or a father
Any role I assume old or new
Am I not a human too?

I can be sad and get upset
I can also be in a cold sweat
Please let us sob and weep
For our feelings sorrowful and deep

You are a boy you can't cry !!!
Before it drips, let your tears dry
Heard this since our young old days
But can we be happy always?

We do need healings
For our unpleasant feelings
Please allow us to vent out our mind
Just as it is, for every womankind.

Summary
Every individual has the right to express their emotions.
But in some societies, males are discouraged from

expressing their sadness overtly. This subdues their emotions and can take an undesirable turn. A weeping male is considered to be weak and emotional by some members of the society. This poem is an appeal on behalf of male fraternity to allow them to cry for venting out their grief, irrespective of their societal role, just as their counterparts (women) are permitted to.

एक बेचारा बाप

सो जा मेरे लाल
अपने बाप का देख तू हाल
अब छोड़ दे रोना
मुझे भी तो है सोना
ना कर मुझे तू बेहाल

"आज तुझको मैं सम्भालूँगा
खाना पीना मैं बनाऊँगा"
ऐसे तेरी माँ से मैंने कहा था
न जाने मुझ पर कौन सा गर्व चढ़ा था
 अब चुप हो जा और तेरे बाप पर कर एहसान

तेरी माँ रखती है सबका खयाल
"दस हाथ है क्या उसके?" मन में मेरे सवाल
काम में उसे सहयोग करेंगे
हमेशा एहसानमंद रहेंगे
कहाँ ममता और करुणा की ऐसी मिसाल?

सारांश

घर और बच्चे संभालना एक कला है जिसमें शायद स्त्रीवर्ग जन्मजात से बहुत निपुण है। इस हास्यकारक कविता में एक बाप अपनी पत्नी से अहंकार में आकर घर और बच्चे संभालने की बात करता है। लेकिन परिस्थिति आने पर वह अस्तव्यस्त हो जाता है और अपने बच्चे से सो जाने की विनती करता है। अपनी गलती महसूस करने पर

वह अपनी पत्नी की प्रशंसा करते हुए उसे सहयोग करने का निश्चय करता है।

Tug of war

On one end of the rope lies the middle age
On the other side of it, is the blooming teenage
Parent-child distance soon seems to be afar
This so called generation gap leads to tug of war

Demand for freedom in the youngster's eyes
Every order of parent, he tends to defies
What an obedient child he was years back !!
Understanding and respect for us
He nowadays seems to lack

I am not a child, I need a freehand
Why don't my parents try to understand?
Whatever I do, my parents find some fault
Each time only I am, offender by default

Let us sit and talk together as and when we can
Do's and don'ts for both sides, we can further plan
Our care and concern, please respect my young one
Our freedom and identity please consider my
experienced one

Summary

The age-old disputes between parents and their teens have been a part of almost every family. These heated debates may even turn out to be a nightmare for both sides. This poem addresses this common issue, naming it as tug of war, and tries to put forth the argument from either part. Being considerate towards the feelings of each other is the solution to the problem as depicted in the poem.

मेरा अस्तित्व

बड़े-बड़े विद्वानों के हाथों ने टटोला
अनेक पंडितों ने मुझे सराहा
अस्थिर होता मेरा मन, जो कभी था अचल
सोचता रहता है 'कहाँ है मेरा अस्तित्व आजकल?'

किसी ने किताब पुकारा तो किसी ने पुस्तक
व्याकुल मन सुनना चाहे वह मानव के हाथों की दस्तक
डर लगता है ना हो जाऊँ धरती से ओझल
सोचता रहता हूँ 'कहाँ है मेरा अस्तित्व आजकल?'

चढ़ती धूल मुझसे हटा दे
फिर से मानव जीवन का हिस्सा बना दे
हमारा नाता रहे हमेशा अटल
कभी मुझे ना हो यह प्रश्न 'कहाँ है मेरा अस्तित्व आजकल?'

सारांश

पुस्तक और किताबों ने अनेक पंडितों और विद्वानों को जन्म दिया है। लेकिन आज मानव जाति इन्हीं से दूर जाती नजर आ रही है। यह दूरी न सहने पर पुस्तक आज मानव जाति से उनके जीवन में फिर से अपना अस्तित्व लाने की बात करती है। इस कविता में पुस्तकों की पीड़ा और मानव जाति से फिर से जुड़ने की अभिलाषा दिखाई गई है।

Love Thy Self

On this swing of life
Looking beyond the facade of existence
I open windows of my mind and discern
'Love thy self'

Purpose of life unveil with light
Ripples of euphoria gushing in me
I hear my soul's soft whisper and sense
'Love Thy Self'

Lucidity of esoteric being
Enlightenment with 'Ikigai'
I feel my ethereal breath within and discover
'Love Thy Self'

Summary
Late middle age or early old age is the phase whereby a person is somewhat relaxed from his family responsibilities. This profound poem depicts the feeling of a person who is in this stage of life and has now found his 'Ikigai (purpose of existence). Earlier he spent his time liking others, but now he believes and feels it's time

he starts loving himself. His realization of self-love is paving the way towards self-fulfillment.

www.ingramcontent.com/pod-product-compliance
Lightning Source LLC
LaVergne TN
LVHW051237200726
843510LV00011B/1594